Playing Musical Bottles

Published in the United States of America by Cherry Lake Publishing
Ann Arbor, Michigan
www.cherrylakepublishing.com

Reading Adviser: Marla Conn MS, Ed., Literacy specialist, Read-Ability, Inc.
Book Design: Jennifer Wahi
Illustrator: Jeff Bane

Library of Congress Cataloging-in-Publication Data

Names: Rowe, Brooke, author.
Title: Playing musical bottles / Brooke Rowe.
Description: Ann Arbor : Cherry Lake Publishing, [2016] | Series: My science
    fun | Audience: K to grade 3.
Identifiers: LCCN 2016016964| ISBN 9781634710282 (hardcover) | ISBN
    9781634712262 (pbk.) | ISBN 9781634711272 (pdf) | ISBN 9781634713252
    (ebook)
Subjects: LCSH: Sound--Experiments--Juvenile literature. | Music--Acoustics
    and physics--Juvenile literature. | Musical
    instruments--Construction--Juvenile literature.
Classification: LCC QC225.5 .R688 2016 | DDC 534.078--dc23
LC record available at https://lccn.loc.gov/2016016964

Printed in the United States of America
Corporate Graphics Inc.

About the illustrator: Jeff Bane and his two business partners own a studio along the American
River in Folsom, California, home of the 1849 Gold Rush. When Jeff's not sketching or illustrating
for clients, he's either swimming or kayaking in the river to relax.

Science Notes

Playing Musical Bottles explores how different pitches of sound are made. In this experiment, glass bottles are filled with water and tapped with a spoon. High and low pitches are a result of sound vibrating in the bottle, the more water in the bottle the lower the pitch.

Do you like **music**? It's fun to dance to music. You can also sing to music.

People make music in many different ways. Some people play the **piano**. Other people play the **guitar**.

Do you think you can make music? Maybe you can find your own special way.

Let's find out!

- 5 matching glass bottles

- Water

- Metal spoon

You will need these things

Line up the bottles. Leave some space between them.

Pour water into the bottles.
Add a different amount of
water to each bottle.

Use the spoon to tap the bottles. Notice the sounds the bottles make.

What do you notice?

You can tap the bottles to make music. You can play a song.

Why do you think this is?

Try adding bottles with new shapes. Add big bottles. Add small bottles. **Compare** the sounds the bottles make.

Try different bottles!

Good job. You're done!
Science is fun!

What new questions do you have?

glossary

compare (kuhm-PAIR) to see what is alike or different about two or more things

guitar (gih-TAHR) an instrument with strings used to make music

music (MYU-zik) sounds that are sung by voices or played by instruments

piano (pee-AN-oh) a large instrument with a keyboard used to make music

index